CLASSIFYING ANIMALS

Fish

Sarah Wilkes

CLASSIFYING ANIMALS

Titles in this series:

Amphibians Birds Fish Insects Mammals Reptiles

Conceived and produced for Hodder Wayland by

Nutshell
MEDIA

Intergen House, 65–67 Western Road, Hove BN3 2JQ, UK
www.nutshellmedialtd.co.uk

Consultant: Jane Mainwaring, Natural History Museum
Editor: Polly Goodman
Designer: Tim Mayer
Illustrator: Jackie Harland
Picture research: Morgan Interactive Ltd and Victoria Coombs

Published in Great Britain in 2006 by Hodder Wayland, an imprint of Hodder Children's Books.

This paperback edition published in 2007 by Wayland, an imprint of Hachette Children's Books

The website addresses (URLs) included in this book were valid at the time of going to press. However, because of the nature of the Internet, it is possible that some addresses may have changed, or sites may have changed or closed down since publication. While the author and publishers regret any inconvenience this may cause the readers, no responsibility for any such changes can be accepted by either the author or the publisher.

British Library Cataloguing in Publication Data
Wilkes, Sarah, 1964–
Fish. – (Classifying animals)
1. Fishes – Classification – Juvenile literature
I. Title
597'.012

ISBN 978 0 7502 5300 0

Cover photograph: an Indo-Pacific Bluetang.
Title page (clockwise from top left): a mudskipper, an angelfish, a viperfish, and a seahorse.
Chapter openers: close-up photographs of the scales of (from top to bottom) a broomtail wrasse, a coral grouper, an emperor angelfish, a sabre squirrelfish and a blue triggerfish.

Picture acknowledgements
Corbis *cover*; **Ecoscene** 4 (Adrian Davies), 5 (Reinhard Dirscheri), 11, 12, 13, 14 (Phillip Colla), 25 (Jeff Collett), 26 (Clive Druett), 27 (Michael Gore), 29, 34 (Reinhard Dirscheri), 35, 36 (Jeff Collett), 37 (Reinhard Dirscheri), 39 (John Liddiard), 41 (Reinhard Dirscheri), 42 (Chinch Gryniewicz), 43 (John Liddiard); **naturepl.com** 6 (Brandon Cole), 7 (Reijo Juurinen/Naturbild), 8 (Florian Graner), 9 (Doug Perrine), 10 (Bruce Rasner), 15 (Georgette Douwma), 17 (Jeff Rotman), 18 (Juan Manuel Borrero), 19 (Doc White), 20 (Doug Perrine), 21 (Doc White), 22 (Chris Gomersall), 23 (Jeff Rotman), 24 (Herman Brehm), 28 (Reijo Juurinen/Naturbild), 30 (top & bottom), 31 Jeff Foott, 32 (Julian Partridge), 33 (Doc White), 38 (Fabio Liverani), 40 (Aflo).

Printed and bound in China.

Hachette Children's Books
338 Euston Road, London NW1 3BH

CONTENTS

WHAT ARE FISH?

FISH ARE FOUND IN ALL THE WATERS OF THE WORLD, FROM frozen polar seas and tropical coral reefs, to rivers and tiny pools. There are about 27,500 species of fish, including great white sharks, eagle rays, salmon, cod and minnows. They range in size from giant whale sharks more than 12 m (39 ft) long to tiny gobies just 1 cm (0.4 in) in length.

Fish features

Fish belong to a large group of animals called vertebrates, along with amphibians, reptiles, birds and mammals. All vertebrates have a vertebral column – a series of small bones that run down their back. All fish have bodies that are adapted to swimming and living in water. Most have a streamlined body that can slip easily through the water and they have paired fins rather than limbs. All fish have a muscular tail that ends in a vertical tail fin, which they use to propel themselves through the water. In most species, the skin is covered in scales. Running along each side of the body is a special sense organ called the lateral line system, which is a line of sensory receptors that are sensitive to pressure. Fish have gills in order to breathe underwater. Water flows through their gills and oxygen passes from the water into their blood.

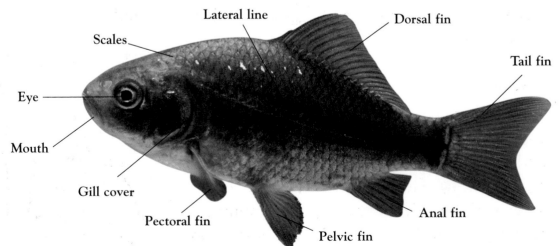

A typical bony fish such as this goldfish (*Carassius auratus*) has two sets of paired fins (pectoral and pelvic), and a number of single fins.

4

CLASSIFICATION

About 2 million different organisms have been identified and sorted into groups, in a process called classification. Biologists look at the similarities and differences between organisms, and group together those with shared characteristics. The largest group is the kingdom, for example the animal kingdom. Each kingdom is divided into smaller groups, called phyla (singular: phylum). Each phylum is divided into classes, which are divided into orders, then families, genera and finally species. A species is a single type of organism with unique features that are different from all other organisms, for example a blue shark. Only members of the same species can reproduce with each other and produce fertile offspring. Sometimes there are extra groups such as subclasses and superorders.

The classification of the blue shark (*Prionace glauca*) is shown on the right.

KINGDOM: Animalia

PHYLUM: Chordata

CLASS: Chondrichthyes

SUBCLASS: Elasmobranchii

ORDER: Carcharhiniformes

FAMILY: Carcharhinidae (Requiem sharks)

GENUS: Prionace

SPECIES: glauca (blue shark)

One way of remembering the order of the different groups is to learn this phrase:
'**K**ings **P**lay **C**hess **O**n **F**ridays **G**enerally **S**peaking'.

Reproduction
Most fish lay eggs in water, which hatch into tiny fish called fry. However, some fish carry their eggs within their body and give birth to live young.

Classes
Fish are classified into one of four classes: hagfish (Myxini), lampreys (Cephalaspidomorphi), cartilaginous fish (Chondrichthyes) and bony fish (Osteichthyes). This book looks at the four classes and the orders within them, examining the features of each and how they differ from one another. It is not possible to cover all the orders of fish in this book. However, there is a complete list of the orders, superorders, subclasses and classes on page 44.

This lizardfish is a type of bony fish. It is a predator and has caught a smaller fish in its mouth.

Jawless Fish (Myxini and Cephalaspidomorphi)

Hagfish are long, slender and pinkish in colour, growing to a length of about 70 cm (28 in). They are best known for the large quantities of sticky slime that they produce.

JAWLESS FISH ARE BIZARRE-looking fish that do not look like other fish. They are an ancient group that first appeared more than 500 million years ago. Jawless fish are divided into two classes: hagfish (Myxini) and lampreys (Cephalaspidomorphi). Only a few species of each survive today.

Shared features

The main feature of jawless fish is their lack of a jaw. In place of a jaw they have a round mouth, a sucker and a rasping tongue. Their bodies are long and look a bit like an eel. They have small fins, none of which are paired. Jawless fish do not have scales covering their skin. Instead they produce large quantities of protective slime, especially the hagfish. Their gills are found inside their body, but there is no gill cover on the outside as in other fish. Instead, their gills open through tiny pores (holes) in the body wall.

Lampreys

Lampreys have a sucker with a fringed edge surrounding their mouth. Instead of a pair of nostrils, they have a single nasal opening, either at the end of their snout or on top of their head. The flexible spine is made of cartilage, which helps lampreys to swim more powerfully. Their brain case is also made of cartilage.

Life cycle of the lamprey

Some lampreys live in fresh water while others, such as the sea lamprey, live in salt water. Both have to breed in fresh water, so sea lampreys have to swim back to freshwater rivers in order to lay their eggs. Lamprey eggs are large and surrounded by a tough egg case. The eggs hatch into larval fish known as ammocete larvae, which bury themselves in mud in fresh water. The larvae look very different from the adult fish and have to undergo metamorphosis to change into adults. Young sea lampreys return to the sea to mature.

Lamprey food

Lampreys are unusual in that the adult fish are parasites. A parasite is an animal that lives on another animal, harming that animal in the process. Lampreys attach themselves to the skin of other fish using their sucker and teeth, and suck their blood. In some places, such as the Great Lakes of North America, lampreys are a serious pest because they harm the fish stocks. Lampreys are not native to the Great Lakes. They were introduced from other parts of the world by being carried in the ballast tanks of ships, which were emptied into the Great Lakes.

Hagfish

The worm-like hagfish lives on the seabed, where it scavenges on the dead bodies of animals. It uses rows of horny teeth on its tongue to rasp at food. Surrounding its mouth is a ring of tentacles. The hagfish eats by pushing its head inside the bodies of rotting animals and sucking the flesh into its mouth.

Adult lampreys attach themselves to fish and marine mammals using a sucker with pointed teeth. Once attached, the lamprey creates a wound on its prey's skin using its rasping tongue and sharp teeth, and feeds on the prey's blood and body tissue. Lampreys grow to about 80 cm (32 in) long.

CARTILAGINOUS FISH (CHONDRICHTHYES)

The ratfish (*Chimaera monstrosa*) lives at depths of 300–500 m (100–200 ft), but it can be found as deep as 1,000 m (400 ft). The first dorsal fin is triangular with a spine in front, whereas the second dorsal fin is long and continuous.

THE GREAT WHITE SHARK IS probably the most frightening of all the fish. This large shark is one of many hundreds of different species of shark, which are grouped together with rays, skates, ratfish and chimeras in a class called cartilaginous fish (Chondrichthyes).

Cartilaginous skeleton

Most vertebrates, such as reptiles, birds and mammals, have a skeleton made from bone. The main characteristic of cartilaginous fish is a skeleton made of cartilage. This is the material that shapes our ears and nose. It is flexible rather than rigid.

There are other features that distinguish cartilaginous fish from other classes of fish. Unlike bony fish, which have a swim bladder filled with air to provide buoyancy, cartilaginous fish do not have a swim bladder. Their oily liver provides a little buoyancy, but they have to keep swimming to stop themselves from sinking.

The skin of cartilaginous fish is rough because it is covered in tiny teeth-like structures, called dermal denticles. Cartilaginous fish have a series of gill slits rather than a single gill cover. They have either five, six or seven slits on each side of their head, through which water is expelled after passing through the gills.

Spiracle

All cartilaginous fish have a spiracle. This is an opening behind the eye. The spiracle in sharks is used to provide oxygenated blood directly to the eye and brain through a separate blood vessel. It is very small or absent in a number of sharks, particularly the fast-swimming sharks. In rays and skates, the spiracle is much larger and is used to actively pump water over the gills, allowing these fish to breathe while buried in the sand (see page 15).

(see page 15)

KEY CHARACTERISTICS
CHONDRICHTHYES

- Skeleton made of cartilage.
- Body covered in dermal denticles.
- Gill slits rather than gill cover.
- Spiracle behind the eye.
- Internal fertilization.
- No swim bladder.
- Asymmetrical tail fin.

Reproduction

Unlike other fish, fertilization in cartilaginous fish is internal. The male fish inserts a pair of organs called claspers into the female to fertilize her eggs. The female then produces a few large eggs. The eggs are supplied with a large yolk, so that by the time the young fish hatch, they are well developed. Since cartilaginous fish only produce a few eggs (between 2 and 300) compared with the thousands produced by bony fish, the females have to be very careful about where they place them. For example, the female Port Jackson shark screws her eggs into rock crevices. The eggs may take up to 15 months to develop. The young sharks are miniature versions of their parents.

Rays and some sharks, for example the lemon shark, do not lay eggs. The females retain the eggs inside their body and give birth to live young, called pups. Species that give birth to live young are called viviparous.

Subclasses

Cartilaginous fish are divided into two subclasses: Holocephali and Elasmobranchii. Holocephali is made up of ratfish and chimeras. Elasmobranchii is far larger and contains the sharks and rays. It is divided into 13 orders.

The lemon shark (*Negaprion brevirostris*) gives birth to live young in shallow nursery grounds between April and September. The pups remain in the nursery grounds for several years before they swim out to the open ocean. This pup is being born tail first.

SHARKS, RAYS AND SKATES (ELASMOBRANCHII)

IN 1976, A TEAM OF RESEARCHERS MADE AN EXCITING discovery. They brought up the body of a gigantic shark measuring 4.5 m (15 ft) in length and weighing just over 750 kg (1,600 lb). It was like no other shark, with a broad head and an extra-wide mouth. Not surprisingly, it was given the name megamouth (*Megachasma pelagios*).

There have been only 30 confirmed sightings of the megamouth (*Megachasma pelagios*) in the Indian, Pacific and Atlantic Oceans.

Sharks, rays and skates belong to the subclass Elasmobranchii. This large group of cartilaginous fish is divided into a number of superorders, including the frilled, cow, dogfish, angel and saw sharks (Squalomorpha); the bullhead, carpet, ground and mackerel sharks (Galeomorpha); and rays and skates (Batoids).

Shark features

There are approximately 360 species of sharks. Most species are about 2.5 m (8 ft) long, but they range in size from the green dogfish, at just 25 cm (10 in) long, to whale sharks, which can grow up to 20 m (66 ft) long. Even though they belong to the same subclass, sharks look very different from rays and skates. Sharks have a streamlined, tapering body with a powerful, muscular tail that powers their swimming. Their tail ends in a distinctive asymmetric tail fin, where the upper lobe is bigger than the lower lobe. Sharks have large, triangular-shaped pectoral fins, held out at right angles to their bodies, which are used for steering and balance. When they swim just under the surface, their dorsal fin sticks out of the water. Another feature of sharks is an eyelid known as the nictitating membrane, which protects the eye.

Internal gills

Sharks have internal gills that take up oxygen from the water. The water enters the mouth and is pushed back over the gills and out through the gill slits. The number of gill slits on the side of the head is a distinguishing feature. Most sharks have five gills but some sharks, including the cow sharks, have six gills. The seven-gill shark is the only species to have seven gill slits.

Shark teeth

Sharks' teeth are a triangular shape, like their scales. They have rows of teeth along their jaws, a bit like a conveyor belt of replacement teeth. As the sharks lose teeth, they are replaced by new ones from behind. On average, a shark's tooth is replaced every seven to eight days.

The great white shark's Latin name, *Carcharodon carcharias*, means 'ragged tooth'. The largest grow to about 7 m (23 ft) in length – that's about the same as two small cars parked end to end, although most are between 4–5 m (13–16 ft) long.

KEY CHARACTERISTICS
ELASMOBRANCHII

- Five or more gill slits.
- Spiracle.

The whale shark (*Rhincodon typus*) grows to lengths of up to 20 m (66 ft). It feeds on plankton by opening and closing its mouth so that water flows through its gill chamber. Plankton is trapped against the dermal denticles that line the gills and the pharynx.

Food

Sharks are highly effective predators, with superbly developed senses to help them find their prey in the water. However the largest shark, the whale shark, is a harmless plankton feeder.

Senses

Sharks have a unique sensor system, called the Ampullae of Lorenzini, which is located in the snout. The sensors in this system can detect electrical signals generated by the muscle movements of prey. They can even detect the movements of fish lying under the sand. In addition to their sensor system, sharks have excellent sight and smell. Their sense of smell is many thousands of times better than that of a person, enabling them to detect one drop of blood in 100 litres (25 gallons) of water.

Prey

Sharks feed on a range of prey animals, including fish, marine mammals and birds. They also scavenge on dead bodies. Sharks that feed near the surface, such as mako and thresher sharks, are streamlined, powerful swimmers. The mako shark, a type of mackerel shark, can swim at speeds of up to 97 km/h (60 mph) in short bursts to catch fast-moving tuna and marlin. The heat generated by muscles in their body and tail warms their blood, which helps them to function well in cold water.

Bottom-feeding shark species, such as horn sharks, tend to be stout, blunt-headed and more sluggish, while shellfish eaters, such as porbeagle sharks, have coarse, crushing teeth.

Plankton feeders

Whale, basking and megamouth sharks feed on plankton. They each have a large, wide mouth and they can take in large quantities of water into their gill chamber. The water is filtered by the gills as it passes out through the gill slit and the plankton is then swallowed. Whale and basking sharks swim across oceans in search of food. The megamouth is different. It lives deep in the ocean and swims up to the surface at night to feed on plankton.

Life cycle

Sharks take from 3 to 16 years to reach sexual maturity, depending on the species. In viviparous sharks, the gestation period ranges from 6 months to 2 years. There is an average of 12 pups in a litter, but there may be as few as one or two.

STRONG SWIMMERS

■ The mako shark holds the speed record for long-distance travel. It is known to swim 2,130 km (1,324 miles) in 37 days, an average of about 58 km (36 miles) per day.

■ The bull shark is also known as the river whaler because it swims up some of the world's largest rivers, such as the Amazon. It has been found more than 3,000 km (1,900 miles) from the sea.

The horn shark (*Heterodontus francisci*) is a bottom-dwelling shark that grows to about 1.2 m (4 ft) in length. It has rounded fins, a blunt snout, ridges over the eyes and a spine that sticks out of the dorsal fin. This one is feeding on squid eggs that cover the seabed.

Rays and skates

Rays and skates look very different from sharks. There are
456 species of rays and skates, divided into five orders: skates
(Rajiformes); guitarfish (Rhinobatiformes); electric rays
(Torpediniformes); stingrays and eagle rays (Myliobatiformes);
and sawfish (Pristiformes).

Flattened bodies

The main feature of rays and skates is a body that is squashed
from top to bottom. The width of their body ranges from just
25 cm (10 in) to 2 m (7 ft). The pectoral fins of rays and skates
are greatly enlarged to look like a pair of wings held out to the
sides of their body. When they swim, these fins gently rise up and
down – a bit like a flapping bird. Their tail is long and slender. In
some species the tail bears sharp, poisonous barbs that can inflict
painful wounds. Some rays are able to produce a severe electric
shock to stun their prey.

**The distinctive markings
on the underside of
mobula and manta rays
are used by biologists to
identify individuals and
allow them to be tracked.
Mobula rays (below) are
smaller than manta rays
and tend to occur in
shoals. There are nine
species of mobula rays.**

Habitat and food

Skates and many rays live on the seabed, where they feed on prey such as crustaceans and worms. Their body is adapted to bottom living. For example, their mouth is located on their lower surface. Their teeth are hard, flattened plates, ideal for crushing the hard shell of invertebrates such as crabs and clams. Another adaptation is the position of their spiracle, which is located on their dorsal (top) surface. If the spiracle was positioned on their ventral (lower) surface, they would get a mouthful of muddy water.

Many rays live in groups, in estuaries and other places where there are sandy seabeds. They are also found in the open ocean and in kelp beds of coastal waters. Rays feed by moving through masses of plankton or shoals of small fish, turning slowly from side to side. They use large flap-like lobes on either side of their head to fan prey into their broad mouth.

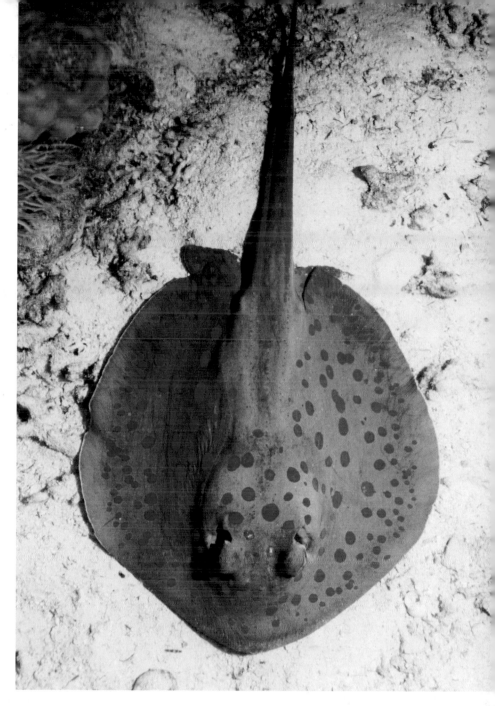

The blue spotted stingray (*Taeniura lymna*) uses two plates in its mouth to crush the shells of crabs, prawns, and molluscs. Its tail is slightly longer than its body and it has a spine (the stinger) about halfway down its tail.

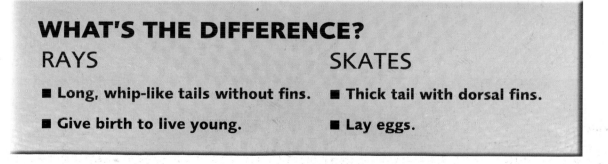

WHAT'S THE DIFFERENCE?

RAYS
- Long, whip-like tails without fins.
- Give birth to live young.

SKATES
- Thick tail with dorsal fins.
- Lay eggs.

Bony Fish (Osteichthyes)

There are more than 24,000 species of bony fish, making Osteichthyes the largest of the four classes of fish. Bony fish are found in every aquatic habitat, and a few species, such as the walking catfish and the mudskipper, are even able to crawl about on land. Bony fish are a major source of food for millions of people.

Bony fish features

The main characteristic of bony fish is the presence of a bony skeleton. They have a swim bladder to help their buoyancy and a single gill cover on each side of their head, called an operculum, rather than gill slits. The gill cover allows a current of water to pass out from the gills during exhalation, but prevents water from entering during inhalation.

Life cycle

Most bony fish lay eggs that hatch within days into tiny fish. However some fish, including common aquarium fish such as guppies, swordtails and mollies, carry the eggs inside their bodies and give birth to live young. Most bony fish do not provide any care for their offspring, but there are a few exceptions. For example, some female African cichlids carry their

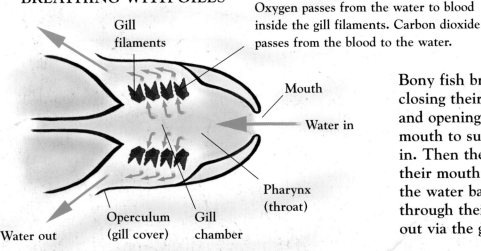

BREATHING WITH GILLS

Gill filaments

Oxygen passes from the water to blood inside the gill filaments. Carbon dioxide passes from the blood to the water.

Mouth

Water in

Pharynx (throat)

Water out

Operculum (gill cover)

Gill chamber

Bony fish breathe by closing their gill cover and opening their mouth to suck water in. Then they close their mouth and force the water back through their gills and out via the gill covers.

eggs and then their young in their mouth. The young fish swim out of the mouth and feed close to the female, but at the first sign of danger, they return to her mouth.

Subclasses

The class of Osteichthyes is divided into two subclasses: Actinopterygii and Sarcopterygii. Actinopterygii are ray-finned fish. Their fins are made from webs of skin supported by bony spines. The paired fins are quite mobile and can be rotated to act as brakes or used for turning. This is different from the pectoral fins of sharks, which have a very limited range of movements. Within Actinopterygii there are two groups: primitive ray-finned fish known as Chondrostei, which includes the paddlefish and gar, and the more advanced ray-finned fish known as Teleostei.

Sarcopterygii

The subclass Sarcopterygii contains primitive fish with fleshy fins. A lobe of bone and muscle extends into their fins. This subclass includes lungfish and the ancient coelacanth. Their fleshy fins are very flexible and in the lungfish they support the body of the fish while it is on land. There are six species of lungfish and a single species of coelacanth. The lungfish is unusual because it has gills and a single lung formed from its swim bladder. A good blood supply to the lung enables this fish to survive out of water for long periods of time. The first specimen of a living coelacanth known to science was caught in a net off the coast of South Africa in 1938. It was nicknamed 'old four legs' because its pectoral and pelvic fins resembled limbs. Until this time, coelocanths were thought to have been extinct for millions of years.

The beautifully coloured queen angelfish (*Holacanthus ciliaris*) has a tall, flat body. It feeds on a variety of marine invertebrates, especially sponges, jellyfish and corals, as well as plankton and algae.

KEY CHARACTERISTICS
OSTEICHTHYES
- Bony skeleton.
- Gill cover or operculum.
- Swim bladder.

17

PRIMITIVE RAY-FINNED FISH (CHONDROSTEI)

PRIMITIVE RAY–FINNED FISH ARE AMONG THE MOST unusual-looking fish within the subclass Actinopterygii. Only found in the northern hemisphere, this superorder is made up of four orders: bichirs (Polypteriformes); sturgeon and paddlefish (Acipenseriformes); gars (Semionotiformes); and bowfins (Amiiformes).

Gars have needle-like teeth and a heavily scaled body. The largest gars grow up to 3.7 m (12 ft) in length.

Chondrostei features

Members of Chondrostei are large fish with a skeleton that is part bone and part cartilage. The skull and some of the fin supports are made of bone, while the body and tail are supported by a cartilaginous backbone. Some species have a shark-like asymmetrical tail fin. Most of these fish lack scales on their body. However, if they are present, the scales are usually diamond shaped and heavy looking. One very distinctive feature of Chondrostei fish is that their backbone turns sharply upward into the upper lobe of the tail fin. Some species have a rostrum, which is an extension from the head past the mouth. It is particularly well developed in the paddlefish.

All primitive ray-finned fish have gills for obtaining oxygen. However, the gar, the bowfin and some of the bichirs have a swim bladder lined with blood vessels which can be used as a lung. This is useful because it can gulp air if the oxygen level of the water falls and the fish cannot obtain enough oxygen through its gills.

Habitat

Most primitive ray-finned fish live in fresh water, for example the bichir, which is found in the Nile and some West African rivers. There are a few saltwater examples, such as the European sturgeon. This fish spends its adult life in the sea, but it migrates over hundreds of kilometres to lay its eggs in freshwater rivers.

Gars are predatory fish that are found in North America. They look a bit like the pike, with their elongated body and long jaws. Gars hang motionless amongst vegetation in the water, waiting for prey animals to pass close by before darting out. Their median fins are positioned far back near their tail fin. This arrangement is like the feathers on an arrow, which helps gars to move fast through the water.

Paddlefish live in large rivers such as the Mississippi, where there is plenty of plankton in the water. They open their mouth and filter the water as it flows through their gills. Paddlefish feed at night. During the day they rest at the bottom of deep rivers.

The European sturgeon (*Acipenser sturio*) can grow up to 4 m (13 ft) long. Its long body is scale-free apart from five rows of sharp bony plates. The sturgeon has a relatively long snout and a toothless mouth with four short barbels which it uses to find food.

EELS (ELOPOMORPHA)

EELS AND THE LESSER–KNOWN HALOSAURS, TARPONS AND tapirfish make up the superorder Elopomorpha. These fish look very different from each other, but they have one thing in common – they all start life as a ribbon–like, leptocephalus larva.

The superorder Elopomorpha is made up of five orders: halosaurs (Albuliformes); eels (Anguilliformes); tarpons (Elopiformes); spiny eels and tapirfish (Notacanthiformes); and swallowers (Saccopharyngiformes).

This yellow-edged moray eel (*Gymnothorax flavimarginatus*) is having its mouth cleaned by a humpback cleaner shrimp. These moray eels hide in crevices in the coral reef and wait for prey to pass close by.

Elopomorpha features

Eels have a long, snake-like body. There are more than 100 vertebrae in their backbone, which make their body incredibly flexible. The dorsal and anal fins are small but they extend along the body. Most eels lack scales. Generally, they have a good sense of smell but their eyesight can be poor, especially in deep-sea species.

Halosaurs are strange-looking deep-sea fish that live at depths of 1,800 m (6,000 ft). They have an elongated body about 55 cm (22 in) long and a pointed snout that extends well in front of the mouth.

Halosaurs are covered in small scales, with enlarged scales along their lateral line. The tarpon has a taller body than eels and halosaurs, and it is covered in huge reflective scales. The last ray of the dorsal fin is extended into a long filament and all the fins are well developed.

Predators

Most members of Elopomorpha are predators. Tarpons are fast swimming and can catch other fish. Halosaurs feed on marine worms, crustaceans and bottom-living invertebrates. Moray eels lie hidden in rock crevices and seize their prey as it passes by, using their sharp teeth to bite and grip. Many moray eels have teeth that are strengthened for crushing shells.

KEY CHARACTERISTICS
ELOPOMORPHA

■ Life cycle involves a leptocephalus larva that undergoes metamorphosis to become an adult.

Life cycle

All the fish in Elopomorpha have a similar, complicated life cycle. Adult European eels live in freshwater rivers. When they are ready to breed, they swim downstream and across the North Atlantic Ocean to an area known as the Sargasso Sea (between Bermuda and the Azores). The journey takes seven months, during which time the eels do not eat. They mate, lay their eggs and die in the Sargasso Sea. The eggs hatch into a larval fish called a leptocephalus larva, which looks nothing like the adult. It is ribbon-like and translucent. The larvae drift in currents that carry them back across the Atlantic, a journey that takes two and a half years. Then they undergo metamorphosis and change into cylindrical 'glass eels' known as elvers, which have fins, scales and pigmentation. The young complete their journey by swimming up rivers to grow into adults.

The bizarre-looking gulper eel grows up to 2 m (6 ft) in length and is found at depths up to 1,900 m (6,200 ft). Its huge mouth can swallow prey much larger than itself and its stomach stretches to accommodate large meals.

HERRING (CLUPEOMORPHA)

HERRING, PILCHARDS AND anchovy are small fish that live in large groups, called shoals. They are an important link in marine food chains. Herring and their relatives belong to the superorder Clupeomorpha, which is made up of a single order, called Clupeiformes.

The Atlantic herring (*Clupea harengus*) has a tail fin with a distinct fork. All the fins are soft and lack spines. The silvery scales scatter light, which helps to camouflage the fish in the water.

Herring features

There are about 360 species in this order, all of which have a similar appearance. Their streamlined body shape allows them to slip through the water with ease. Their bodies are covered in large scales and the fins are well developed. Many are silver in colour. Herring, pilchards and anchovy are known to have good hearing. This is due to the swim bladder being linked to the ear, which increases their sensitivity to sound.

Life cycle

Atlantic herring return to the same spawning grounds each year to lay their eggs. Large shoals collect in the spawning grounds and each female lays up to 40,000 tiny eggs, which are fertilized by the males.

KEY CHARACTERISTICS
CLUPEOMORPHA

- Body covered by large scales.
- Swim bladder linked to the ear to improve hearing.
- Live in shoals.
- Filter feeders.

The eggs sink to the seabed, where they hatch into minute larvae that look a bit like tiny eels. The larvae swim to the upper layers of the ocean, where they feed on tiny animal plankton and eggs. Only a few survive to become adults.

Food chains

Herring, pilchards and anchovy are filter feeders, feeding on animal plankton in the water. They open their large mouths and sieve food from the water. Animal plankton spend the daylight hours in deep water and migrate to the surface to feed in the safety of darkness. Herring and their relatives have learnt to follow this movement of their food, so each day they migrate from the depths to the surface, too.

Threats

Herring, pilchards and anchovy live in large shoals, so they attract the attention of many predatory fish such as salmon, tuna and marlin. They are also eaten by seals, dolphins and seabirds. Anchovy and herring are important commercial fish and they are caught by trawlers around the world. Unfortunately they have been overfished and their numbers are falling. This is affecting the other animals in the food chain that rely on them for food.

SHOALS

A shoal is made up of many fish but it acts as an individual. In a shoal, each fish swims parallel to its neighbour, using sight, hearing and its lateral line to keep in position, staying with the rest of the shoal even as it twists and turns. Only bony fish can shoal like this. Fish swim in shoals because it is safer to swim in a group than alone. Predators find it difficult to follow a single fish in a shoal because they are distracted by the others.

Anchovy (*Engraulis sp.*) are small, silvery fish with blue-green backs, never growing larger than 20 cm (8 in).

CATFISH (OSTARIOPHYSI)

CATFISH AND THEIR RELATIVES LIVE MOSTLY IN FRESHWATER lakes, rivers and streams. They belong to the superorder Ostariophysi, which is made up of about 6,000 species divided into five orders: milkfish; minnows and carp; characins, tigerfish, tetras and piranha; electric eels and knifefish; and catfish.

Ostariophysi features

Despite their varied appearance, the fish in this superorder are classed together because they have an internal feature in common. This is the Weberian apparatus – an unusual arrangement of bones in their vertebral column that transmits sounds from the swim bladder to the inner ear. The Weberian apparatus gives these fish excellent hearing. Milkfish have a slightly different arrangement.

ELECTRIC EEL

The electric eel has an organ in its body that can produce electricity. Despite its name, the electric eel is not an eel but a type of knifefish. This large fish has a long fin running along its underside and a tail that tapers to a point. Electric eels have poor eyesight. They find their way around by producing weak pulses of electricity. They also use their electric organs to produce bolts of electricity, which are powerful enough to kill their prey and even humans.

The electric eel (*Electrophorus electricus*) is found in the Amazon River basin in South America, where it prefers marshy or stagnant areas. This one has been fished from a river.

Instead of a Weberian apparatus, milkfish have modified ribs, which transmit sounds from the swim bladder to the ear. Sound is important to many fish in Ostariophysi and it is often used to communicate with other fish.

The striped catfish (*Plotosus lineatus*) has a striped body that tapers toward its tail. It grows to about 35 cm (14 in) long. Juvenile striped catfish often form shoals.

Catfish

Catfish have a flattened head and barbels. A barbel is a bit like a whisker and it is covered in taste buds to help the fish to find food. Catfish have poor eyesight but since they often live in murky water, it does not matter too much. Most have a smooth, scaleless skin although a few species, such as the bushy mouth catfish, are exceptions. The bushy mouth catfish has enlarged scales that look like plates of armour. The majority of catfish have sharp pectoral and dorsal spines, and in some species these spines can release poisons. Many catfish release an alarm substance when injured, which sends a signal to others in the vicinity to flee.

KEY CHARACTERISTICS
OSTARIOPHYSI

■ **Most species have the Weberian apparatus for hearing.**

■ **Catfish have barbels and most have a scaleless skin.**

Carp

Carp are deep-bodied, freshwater fish. They have been introduced to rivers, ponds and lakes around the world as a source of food. The carp has a highly mobile mouth, which can extend to rummage through mud and sediment on the bottom of ponds and lakes in the search for food. There are no teeth on the jaws. The fish grinds its food using teeth in the back of the throat.

Catfish, such as this channel catfish (*Ictalurus punctatus*) from North America, use the barbels around their mouth to find food in murky water.

Feeding

Many members of the catfish superorder, such as tetras, hatchet fish and zebrafish, are kept in home aquariums because they are colourful and easy to keep. Their natural habitat is tropical rivers, where they move around in shoals for safety, feeding on plankton and plants. They in turn are eaten by larger predatory fish as well as birds, so these fish perform an important role in the food web of rivers.

Most of the catfish superorder are either predators or scavengers. Catfish live on the sea and river floor. They are nocturnal fish (active at night) and feed alone, relying on their sense of touch and hearing to navigate. The wels is the largest of the catfish. It has two extra-long barbels on its upper jaw and four smaller ones on its lower jaw. Like all catfish, it uses taste buds on its barbels to find food in the gloom. It is a predator that feeds on crustaceans, small fish, ducks, small geese and even otters.

Tigerfish are large predators that form shoals in African rivers. They grow up to 1.8 m (6 ft) long. These fish catch and swallow their prey whole, head first. They can tackle prey up to half their own length.

Piranhas

Most varieties of piranhas are harmless, eating water plants, fruits and seeds. However, the red-bellied piranhas are aggressive predators. Their small, sharp, triangular teeth are well spaced out so that when the jaw closes, the teeth interlink and they can slice off bits of their prey. The lower jaw sticks out in front of the upper jaw and gives the fish a strong bite. Piranhas feed at dawn and at dusk. They wait, hidden in the shadows, until they detect prey and dart forwards to catch it. Most of their prey are small fish and insects, but they also attack larger animals such as sloths, capybaras and deer when they fall in the water from trees or while crossing rivers.

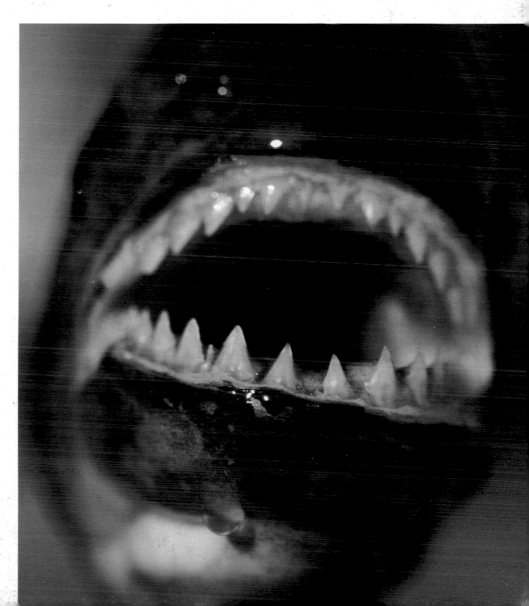

The teeth of the piranha are triangular with razor-sharp edges. The large, powerful lower jaw sticks out beyond the upper jaw so that the teeth fit together like a trap. The piranha rips the body of its prey into small pieces.

Salmon (Protacanthopterygii)

Salmon and their relatives are large, powerful predatory fish that are found around the world. The superorder Protacanthopterygii includes salmon, trout, char, pike and hatchet fish. It is made up of three orders: salmon and trout; pikes; and argentines and smelts.

The brown trout (*Salmo trutta fario*) lives in rivers, where it feeds on insects, crayfish, molluscs, frogs and rodents. It spawns between late autumn and early winter in shallow rivers with a gravel bed. The female digs a nest in the gravel and lays about 2,000 eggs.

Salmon features

The fish in this superorder are characterized by their long bodies, powerful, muscular tails and large tail fins. Their bodies are streamlined and there are few, if any, scales. Their fins are small and do not stick out much so they do not slow the fish down. Their pelvic fins are positioned well back on the body and there is a small, fleshy fin located on the upper edge near the tail, called the adipose fin. The arrangement of fins on these fish is ideally suited to the way they feed because they tend to ambush their prey, shooting forwards with a burst of speed.

Predators

Salmon and their relatives are mostly predatory, so they have a long jaw and sharp teeth for catching prey. The teeth of the pike are particularly large and this fish is renowned for swallowing prey almost half its own size. The hatchet fish is a deep-sea fish with a very tall body. It feeds mostly on invertebrates, which it sucks into its wide mouth. There is little food in the depths of the ocean, so these fish need to be able to swallow any prey they find, however large.

Spook fish

Spook fish (*Dolichopteryx binocularis*) are bizarre-looking deep-sea fish. Their pectoral fins are greatly extended to half the length of their body. This fish gets its name from its strange, tubular-shaped eyes, which resemble a pair of binoculars and enable it to see the area above its head. Spook fish have a second pair of eyes, located on the side of the tubular eyes, for side vision.

Life cycle

Some members of the salmon superorder, such as the pike and grayling, live in fresh water for their entire life. Others, such as the capelin, live in salt water. Capelin live in shoals and live for most of the year in the Arctic Ocean. They migrate to coastal waters, where they spawn on beaches. The eggs are laid at high tide in the sand and become buried. This protects the eggs and then at the next high tide, the young fish hatch and swim out to sea. A few species, such as the salmon, trout and eulachon, have a life cycle that involves fresh and salt water (see pages 30–31).

The pike (*Esox luciu*) is a predatory fish that lives in fresh water. It lurks amongst the weeds, waiting for prey to pass by. Pikes eat mainly fish, but they also catch water voles and ducklings. They grow up to 150 cm (60 in) in length and weigh up to 25 kg (55 lb).

The eyes of the salmon embryos are just visible inside these eggs. Only a few eggs survive to adulthood. Many are not fertilized, or are washed away, or covered by mud.

(Below) The male sockeye salmon (*Oncorhynchus nerka*), below left, has a hooked jaw and a humped back, while the female (below right) has a more rounded body.

Salmon life cycle

Salmon make one of the most amazing journeys seen in the animal world. These large, active fish travel from fresh water to the sea and then back to fresh water to complete their life cycle. All species of salmon undergo a similar journey. The one featured on this page is the journey of the sockeye salmon, which breeds in rivers along the Pacific coast of North America and lives its adult life in the northern Pacific Ocean. The sockeye salmon is also called the red or blue back salmon.

Migration

The life cycle of the sockeye salmon starts when the breeding adults return to the rivers in which they were born. They swim up the rivers to the breeding grounds, often overcoming obstacles such as rapids, waterfalls and fallen trees. Scientists are uncertain how salmon navigate back to their spawning grounds. It may involve their highly developed sense of smell, or an ability to work out direction from the stars. When they are ready to breed, the adult salmon change their appearance. Both sexes gain a bottle-green head and the sides of their bodies turn bright red. The male develops a hump back and hooked jaw.

Alevins (newly hatched salmon) have an enormous yolk sac, which provides all the nutrition they need for the first weeks of their lives. Alevins remain in the redd (nest) until their yolk sac is absorbed. Then they become free-swimming fry (young fish). Alevins need cold, clear, oxygen-rich water to remain healthy. They are preyed upon by aquatic insects and other fish.

Spawning takes place in shallow waters, where there is gravel on the riverbed. The female uses her tail to dig out a nest, called a redd, in the gravel. She lays up to 4,500 tiny eggs, which are fertilized by the male. After spawning, the adult salmon die.

Young fish

The eggs hatch after about 60 days. The tiny fish are called alevins and they grow rapidly. They stay in the gravel for about four months before starting their journey downstream. Sockeye salmon breed only in rivers that drain into a lake. The young fish can spend a year growing, reaching about 10 cm (4 in) long. After a year the older fish, called fingerlings, complete their journey by swimming down to the sea. At this point their body has to undergo changes in order to live in salt water. They spend three to four years in the North Pacific Ocean feeding and maturing. Then, when they are about four years old, they are ready to breed.

SPAWNING

Sockeye and chinook salmon swim as far as 1,600 km (1,000 miles) upstream to spawn, whereas chum, coho and pink salmon spawn closer to the sea. Kokanee salmon live their entire lives in freshwater lakes. Some kokanee spawn in streams that feed into the lake, while others spawn in the shallow water along the lake shore. Like the sockeye salmon, the kokanee and Pacific salmon die after spawning, whereas Atlantic salmon do not.

Jellynose Fish and Dragonfish (Sternopterygii)

JELLYNOSE FISH AND dragonfish live in the depths of the oceans. This is a very inhospitable habitat because it is pitch dark, cold and under high pressure. Jellynose fish and dragonfish are specially adapted to survive in this environment.

The viperfish is one of the fiercest predators of the deep. It has a large mouth and sharp, fang-like teeth. The teeth are so long that they do not fit inside its mouth. It is thought that the viperfish impales its prey on its teeth by swimming at it at high speeds.

Sternopterygii features

The superorder Sternopterygii consists of two orders: jellynose fish (Ateleopodiformes); and dragonfish and viperfish (Stomiiformes). These deep-sea fish have a strange appearance. Jellynose fish have an elongated, quite flabby body. They live on the deep seabed. Dragonfish and viperfish have an elongated body too, with an extra-large head and jaws that can open extremely wide. Their teeth are like needles. All these fish have dark bodies with a velvety skin lacking scales. Many have the ability to produce an eerie light from special organs.

Surviving the deep

One of the main problems of living in the depths of the ocean is the lack of food. It is too dark for plants to grow, so few animals live there. Those that do have to be able to catch and feed on any food they find. This means that they often have large, flexible jaws to swallow whole prey, and huge stomachs. Often their stomach is so large that their heart and gills are pushed backwards as the stomach fills up. Their sharp teeth help them grip their prey.

Some deep-sea fish have special ways of luring their prey. The deep ocean is totally dark, so these fish make their own light using light-producing organs called photophores. Dragonfish have photophores along their sides and around their mouth. They also have a small filament that extends over their mouth with a photophore at the end. They wave the filament around to attract prey.

Extra order: lizardfish (Cyclosquamata)

Cyclosquamata is a superorder of relatively small fish up to about 50 cm (20 in) long. They are named after their lizard-like appearance. Lizardfish sit on the seabed, propped up by their stiff pectoral fins. Their mottled body blends well with the seabed, especially on coral reefs.

Jellynose fish have a mostly cartilaginous skeleton even though they are bony fish. They have a large head with a bulbous nose and a long body that tapers towards the tail. Jellynose fish range in size with the longest reaching up to 2 m (7 ft) in length.

COD AND ANGLERFISH (PARACANTHOPTERYGII)

The single barbel on the chin of this Atlantic cod (*Gadus morhua*) is clearly visible. Cod grow up to 130 cm (51 in) long and weigh as much as 35 kg (77 lb).

COD AND ANGLERFISH BELONG to the superorder Paracanthopterygii. This is a very diverse group of fish. It includes cod, one of the most economically important fish in the world, along with other commercially fished species such as hake, haddock and whiting. It also includes a group of weird bottom-living fish called anglerfish and frogfish. Many of the fish that belong to this superorder are found on the seabed. The commercial fish form large shoals.

Paracanthopterygii features

Most members of Paracanthopterygii have a long and relatively narrow body. One distinctive feature is the arrangement of the fins. The dorsal fin is divided into three sections, while the pelvic and anal fins are positioned well forward. The mouth is usually found on the ventral surface, where it is ideally positioned for bottom feeding. Many species in this superorder have a single barbel on their chin, which is covered in taste buds.

Food chains

Cod is an important part of the marine food chain. Huge shoals of cod swim just above the seabed, feeding on smaller fish such as capelin and herring. The cod are preyed upon by seals, dolphins, and predatory fish such as marlin.

Cod life cycle

Adult cod form large shoals and migrate between their breeding grounds and feeding grounds, following regular routes. This makes the shoals easy to find and catch in fishing nets. Cod breed in spring. A single female cod is thought to lay at least a million eggs, which are fertilized by the males. She lays such a large number of eggs because the survival rates are very low, and only a small number of eggs hatch and grow to adulthood. The large number of eggs attracts many predators that feed on them.

Frogfish and anglerfish

These strange-looking relatives of cod have a patterned body that is camouflaged on the seabed. Frogfish even have an irregular outline, so it is difficult to make out their shape when they are still. Anglerfish are named after their dangling lure – a modified part of their dorsal fin that hangs in front of their mouth to attract prey.

KEY CHARACTERISTICS
PARACANTHOPTERYGII

- Most have a long and relatively narrow body.
- Dorsal fin is divided into three sections.
- Pelvic and anal fins are positioned well forward on the body.
- Ventrally positioned mouth.
- Many have a single barbel on their chin.

The frogfish (*Antennarius sp.*) has a thick skin covered in scales called dermal spicules, which resemble the warts of a toad. Frogfish live in sponges in shallow waters around coral reefs. They use their pectoral and pelvic fins to 'walk' slowly across the reefs.

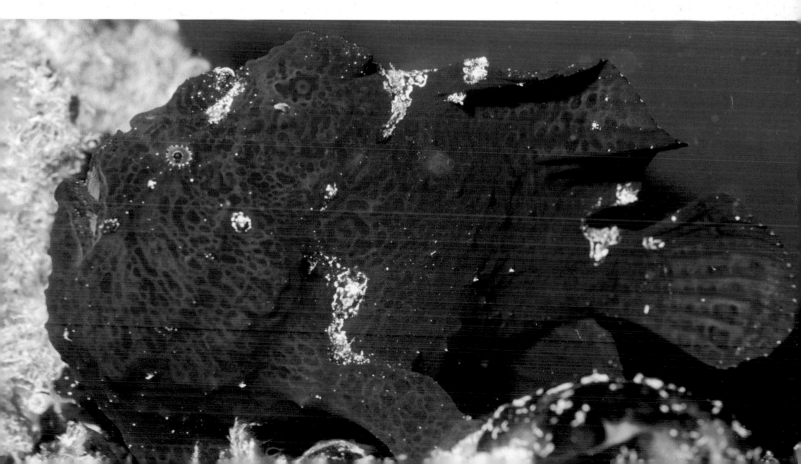

SPINY-RAYED FISH (ACANTHOPTERYGII)

This ragged fin lionfish (*Pterois antennata*) has a striped body and fan-shaped fins. The fins are tipped with spines that can inject a poison.

MORE THAN HALF OF ALL fish species belong to the superorder Acanthopterygii – the spiny-rayed fish. This varied group contains 13 orders of fish including the seahorse, grouper, perch, angelfish, clownfish and plaice.

Spiny-rayed features

Spiny-rayed fish are characterized by the presence of stiff, bony spines that form the front edge of the dorsal and anal fins. In some fish, such as lionfish, these spines are armed with poison. Their paired pelvic fins are positioned far forwards along the body so that the pectoral and pelvic fins are in contact. The scales of these fish have tiny spines that give the surface a rough texture. In a few species, the scales are enlarged to form bony plates, while others have long spines. However a few species have lost their scales altogether. Spiny-rayed fish have a mouth that can be extended and is very mobile.

Body shapes

The body shapes of the fish within this superorder are very varied. Flat fish have a flattened body that looks as if it is lying on one side. Both eyes are on the upper surface. This body shape appears during the development of the larvae. For the first six weeks or so the larvae look much like other fish larvae. Then they start to change shape. Their body becomes flatter and one of the eyes moves across the head so that both eyes lie close together. The upper side of the body becomes darker and speckled, providing camouflage when the fish lies on the seabed.

Another odd-shaped fish is the seahorse. This fish has a long snout, a body covered in spiny scales and a long, prehensile tail. Among the giant species is the ocean sunfish. This is the world's heaviest fish and it looks almost circular when viewed from the side. It has large, triangular dorsal and anal fins, which are held out like blades.

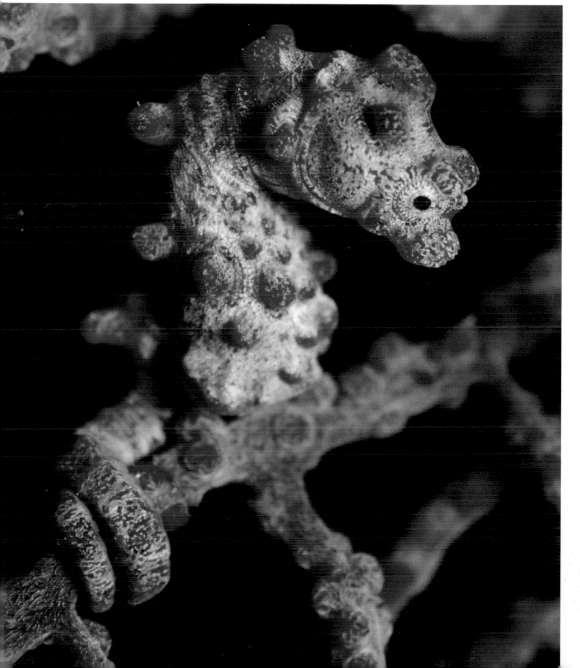

Seahorses are covered in armour-like scales and they swim upright, propelled by tiny fins. This pygmy seahorse (*Hippocampus bargibanti*) is perfectly camouflaged against the coral in which it lives. It is tiny – just 2 cm (0.8 in) long.

Habitat

Most spiny-rayed fish are marine (live in salt water). They are found in coastal waters, coral reefs and in the open ocean. A few, such as mudskippers, live on muddy beaches and can move from pool to pool across the sand.

The mudskipper (*Periophthalmus sp.*) has a large head with bulging eyes. It can flip across the sand from one rock pool to another, breathing through its skin when it is out of water. There are several species of mudskipper, the largest reaching 25 cm (10 in) in length.

Food chains

Spiny-rayed fish play an important role in marine food chains. Their larvae form part of the plankton and are eaten by large invertebrates, other fish and whales. Grunions, for example, feed on the plankton and are themselves preyed upon by larger fish.

Some fast-swimming predators are members of this superorder, including tuna, marlin, swordfish and barracuda. Tuna have a long, streamlined body, sickle-shaped pectoral fins and a crescent-shaped tail. The dorsal fin can be lowered into a groove to increase the streamlining and speed. Heat generated by the muscles as the tuna swim is used to keep the body warm, so they can be active in cold water. Tuna swim thousands of kilometres across the open oceans in search of shoals of anchovy, herring and other fish.

Flying fish live near the surface feeding on plankton. They have an unusual way of escaping from predators such as tuna and marlin. They swim at speeds of up to 60 km/h (37 mph) in the water and propel themselves into the air. Their paired fins are stiff and enlarged so that they can glide over the water for up to 200 m (700 ft).

Camouflage

Many spiny-rayed fish are camouflaged to avoid their predators. The sea dragon has leafy flaps attached to its fins to break up its outline and give it a completely different appearance. Stonefish are slow-moving predators found near the seabed. They have a coloured, scaleless body that blends in with the colour of a rocky seabed. Stonefish have 13 dorsal spines loaded with poison to protect themselves from predators.

The wolffish (*Anarhichas lupus*) is a solitary fish that hides in crevices among rocks. It grabs animals such as crabs, sea urchins and starfish that pass by. Its jaws are exceptionally strong and are equipped with massive teeth to crush the body of its prey.

SIAMESE FIGHTING FISH

The male Siamese fighting fish is fiercely territorial and will fight another male to death in order to defend his territory or win a female. If another male approaches, the fish opens its large, colourful fins to give the impression of being bigger, and its colours become more intense.

When a male is ready to mate, he builds a bubble nest for the eggs by carrying air in his mouth, coating it with saliva and spitting it out in bubbles, which stick together on the surface of the water.

On the Coral Reef

Coral reefs are one of the most diverse habitats in the world. As well as being home to many different types of invertebrates, coral reefs are important fish habitats.

Coral reefs are built by tiny animals, called corals, which are related to the sea anemone. The corals build a limestone skeleton around themselves. When they die, the skeleton is left behind. Coral reefs are found in warm, coastal waters in tropical regions of the world. The water has to be clear and unpolluted for the corals to survive. The largest coral reef is the Great Barrier Reef, off the coast of Australia. There is another long barrier reef off the coast of Belize, in Central America.

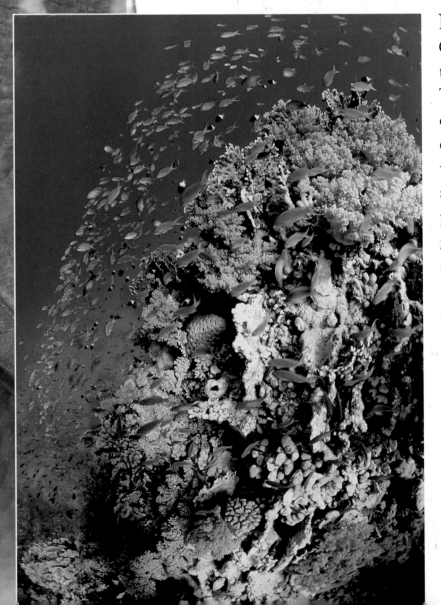

Fish habitat

Coral reefs are home to many fish, from the largest sharks to the smallest gobies. They are excellent fish habitats because of the plentiful food supply, for example, parrot fish feed on the corals while sharks hunt small fish. Coral reefs also provide places to hide from predators. Shoals of small fish, such as glass fish, anthias and bigeyes, swim around the corals. The presence of large numbers of invertebrates and shoals of small fish attract predators, especially sharks that patrol the reef looking for prey. Solitary fish such as moray eels lurk in crevices, while groupers swim close to the reefs, staying in the same area for many years.

Fish are among the most common animals on a coral reef. Shoals of brightly coloured fish swim over the coral while moray eels lurk in crevices. The small fish attract predators such as sharks.

The pink anemonefish (*Amphiprion perideraion*) lives among sea anemones, which are marine animals that look like flowers. The sea anemone provides the fish with protection, since few predators venture near its stinging tentacles. Some anemonefish have natural protection against the stings of the sea anemone, but the pink anemonefish simply has to endure the stings in order to live in the sea anemone.

Some fish have a mutualistic relationship with the coral animals. In this type of relationship, both animals benefit from the association. For example, the clown anemone fish lives amongst the poisonous tentacles of the sea anemone. The fish is immune to the poison due to a layer of mucus over its scales. The sea anemone provides the clown anemone fish with shelter and safety from predators. In return, it feeds on scraps of food left by the fish.

Mangrove swamps

Another important fish habitat are mangrove swamps, which are found along tropical coasts, often near coral reefs. Mangroves are important fish nurseries. It is here that many coral reef fish come to breed. The young fish grow up in the nutrient-rich environment of the swamps before swimming out to the reef as adults. Mangroves are also important to the survival of the reef itself because the roots of the mangrove trees trap silt carried in rivers and stop it from being carried out to sea and covering the corals.

REEF FACTS

- Coral reefs provide a home for more than a quarter of all marine life, yet they take up less than 1% of the ocean floor.

- Coral reefs attract thousands of visitors and bring a lot of money into an area. The value of coral reef tourism is 27 times that of the world's marine fisheries – a very good reason for conserving them!

UNDER THREAT

SADLY FISH, LIKE MANY OTHER TYPES OF ANIMALS, ARE affected by water pollution, loss of habitat and global warming. Overfishing is also a major problem all around the world.

Pollution

Rivers, seas and oceans have long been used as dumping grounds for all sorts of waste, including rubbish, sewage, chemical and radioactive waste. The waste pollutes the water. Fish are active animals and any pollutant that reduces the oxygen content of the water will harm or kill them.

Coral reefs

Coral reefs are extremely sensitive to pollution because they are easily damaged by changes in water quality. They are also sensitive to the temperature of the water and even the slightest change can kill the corals, which leads to fish death. Diving is becoming an increasingly popular activity. Thousands of divers visit coral reefs each day. However, simply touching a

A spill of detergent off the coast has produced a mass of foam that has smothered this rocky shore. Chemical spills kill many of the invertebrate animals living in shallow coastal waters.

coral or brushing a flipper against a coral can do much harm. More divers also means more hotels, dive centres and dive boats. All of this extra tourism is putting the coral reefs under pressure.

Overfishing

Fish are being overfished everywhere. This means that too many fish are being caught and fish stocks are being depleted. The number of Atlantic cod is so low that this species is now classed as endangered. Sharks are also overfished. Often, sharks are caught just so their fins can be chopped off and used in shark fin soup. While the animal is still alive, the rest of the body is then dumped back into the sea. Sharks take a long time to mature and they do not produce many eggs or young, so overfishing reduces their populations rapidly.

Pets

Attractive fish species are popular pets kept in home aquariums. Some of these species are bred specially for this purpose, but far too many are caught in the wild and sold in pet shops.

Conservation

So what can be done? On some coral reefs, certain areas are off-limits to people so the reef is not disturbed. Mangroves can be re-established along tropical coastlines to increase fish breeding areas. Overfishing can be controlled by laws limiting the size of the holes in fishing nets so that young fish can escape and breed. Laws can also ban fishing around fish breeding grounds and even the fishing of certain species, such as Atlantic cod and ice fish. Shark fishing has been carefully regulated in the coastal waters around the USA and the European Union. When fish stocks get really low, the only way to protect them will be to ban fishing altogether.

Some of the more accessible coral reefs are being damaged by scuba divers. Corals are easily damaged by careless flippers and fish are scared away by the constant stream of divers.

SHARK FISHING

Around the world, shark catches are on the increase, mostly because of the demand for their fins in shark fin soup and in various natural medicines. The worldwide catch of shark, skate and ray is more than 800,000 tonnes per year – that's about 70 million individual sharks. For this reason many nations are banning the fishing of sharks. For example, in 2005 the Costa Rican government banned all shark finning and imposed fines and jail terms for anybody caught landing shark fins at Costa Rican ports.

FISH CLASSIFICATION

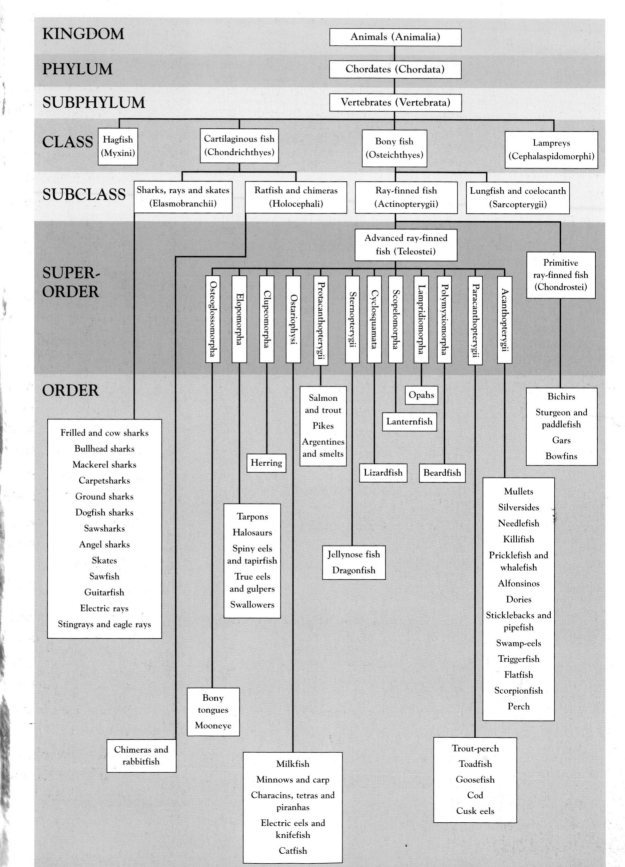

KINGDOM		Animals (Animalia)
PHYLUM		Chordates (Chordata)
SUBPHYLUM		Vertebrates (Vertebrata)

CLASS
- Hagfish (Myxini)
- Cartilaginous fish (Chondrichthyes)
- Bony fish (Osteichthyes)
- Lampreys (Cephalaspidomorphi)

SUBCLASS
- Sharks, rays and skates (Elasmobranchii)
- Ratfish and chimeras (Holocephali)
- Ray-finned fish (Actinopterygii)
- Lungfish and coelocanth (Sarcopterygii)

Advanced ray-finned fish (Teleostei)

SUPER-ORDER
- Osteoglossomorpha
- Elopomorpha
- Clupeomorpha
- Ostariophysi
- Protacanthopterygii
- Sternopterygii
- Cyclosquamata
- Scopelomorpha
- Lampridiomorpha
- Polymyxiomorpha
- Paracanthopterygii
- Acanthopterygii
- Primitive ray-finned fish (Chondrostei)

ORDER

Frilled and cow sharks
Bullhead sharks
Mackerel sharks
Carpetsharks
Ground sharks
Dogfish sharks
Sawsharks
Angel sharks
Skates
Sawfish
Guitarfish
Electric rays
Stingrays and eagle rays

Chimeras and rabbitfish

Bony tongues
Mooneye

Tarpons
Halosaurs
Spiny eels and tapirfish
True eels and gulpers
Swallowers

Herring

Milkfish
Minnows and carp
Characins, tetras and piranhas
Electric eels and knifefish
Catfish

Salmon and trout
Pikes
Argentines and smelts

Jellynose fish
Dragonfish

Lizardfish

Opahs
Lanternfish

Beardfish

Trout-perch
Toadfish
Goosefish
Cod
Cusk eels

Mullets
Silversides
Needlefish
Killifish
Pricklefish and whalefish
Alfonsinos
Dories
Sticklebacks and pipefish
Swamp-eels
Triggerfish
Flatfish
Scorpionfish
Perch

Bichirs
Sturgeon and paddlefish
Gars
Bowfins

Glossary

adapted Changed in order to cope with the environment.

anal fin Single fin on the underside of the fish, in front of the tail fin.

aquatic Living in water.

barbel A whisker-like structure on the snout of a fish, usually covered in taste buds.

buoyancy The ability to remain afloat in a liquid.

camouflage Colours and patterns that allow an animal to blend in with its background.

cartilage Supporting material that is flexible, forming the skeleton of rays and sharks.

cartilaginous Having a skeleton made of cartilage.

crustaceans Animals with a heavy exoskeleton and jointed limbs, for example crabs and lobsters.

dermal denticles Tiny, toothlike projections of skin on cartilaginous fish.

dorsal Related to or situated near or on the back of an animal.

dorsal fin The single fin on the back of a fish.

endangered Animals or plants that are at risk of becoming extinct.

estuary The place where a river enters the sea.

extinct Permanently disappeared.

fertilization The joining of an egg and sperm to produce a new living thing.

filament A thin, threadlike object or fibre.

fin A thin flap of skin supported by spines, found in fish and used to swim, balance and steer.

fish stocks The number of fish in a particular area.

fry Newly hatched fish.

gestation period The time between mating and giving birth, during which the unborn offspring develop inside the body of the mother.

gill An organ used to breathe under water.

gill cover A flap that covers and protects the gills.

invertebrate An animal that does not have a backbone, such as a snail or insect.

kelp bed A thick growth of seaweeds known as kelp, found in coastal waters from depths of 2–30 m. The long fronds of seaweeds are home to many fish and other marine animals.

larva A young animal that changes in body shape to become an adult.

lateral line A line of sensors that runs from behind the head along the side of the body of a fish.

lobe A rounded part of a fin.

median fins The dorsal, anal and caudal fins (the horizontal fins).

metamorphosis A change in body shape during an animal's life cycle.

migrate To make a regular journey to a new habitat.

nictitating membrane The third eyelid of a shark that is transparent and protects the eye.

GLOSSARY

order A category of organisms, ranking above a family and below a class.

parasites Organisms that live on or in another animal or plant, called the host, causing harm to the host.

pectoral fins Paired fins that are found attached to the pectoral girdle of the skeleton.

pelvic fins Paired fins that are found attached to the pelvic girdle of the skeleton.

pharynx The throat.

photophore A light-producing organ found on some fish that live in the deep ocean.

plankton Tiny plants and animals that float in the upper layers of the ocean.

predator An animal that catches and kills other animals.

prehensile Something that can wrap around things to hold on to them, for example the tail of a seahorse.

prey An animal that is caught and killed by a predator.

primitive At an early stage of development.

receptor Something that is able to respond to an external stimulus, such as light.

rostrum On fish, a body part that extends from the head beyond the mouth.

scavenge To feed on dead and decaying bodies.

sensory receptors Structures that recognize a change in the environment, for example nerve endings in the skin that detect heat, cold or pain.

shoal A group of fish.

skeleton The framework of an animal. Some skeletons are made of bones, others of cartilage.

sp. An abbreviation for 'species', used in the Latin names for animals where the exact species is unknown.

spiracle A hole behind the eyes of cartilaginous fish.

streamlined A shape that moves easily through water.

subclass A category of organisms, ranking above an order and below a class.

superorder A category of organisms, ranking above an order and below a subclass.

tentacles Long, usually sensitive extensions from the bodies of some animals, mostly from the head or near the mouth.

translucent Semi-transparent, allowing some light to pass through.

tropical Relating to places near the Equator that have hot and humid weather for much of the year.

ventral surface The lower surface of the body of an animal.

vertebrate An animal that has a backbone.

viviparous Animals that give birth to live young.

yolk The portion of an egg that consists of protein and fat from which the embryo gets its nourishment.

FURTHER INFORMATION

Books

Animal: The Definitive Visual Guide to the World's Wildlife editor David Burnie (Dorling Kindersley, 2004)

Animal Classification by Polly Goodman (Wayland, 2007)

Animal Kingdom: Fish by Sally Morgan (Raintree, 2005)

The Blue Planet by Andrew Byatt, Alastair Fothergill and Martha Holmes (BBC Books, 2001)

Classifying Living Things: Classifying Fish by Louise A. Spilsbury (Heinemann Library, 2003)

DK Animal Encyclopedia (Dorling Kindersley, 2006)

Incredible Creatures: Incredible Fish by John Townsend (Raintree, 2005)

Life Processes series: *Classification* by Holly Wallace (Heinemann Library, 2006)

Nature Files series: *Animal Groupings* by Anita Ganeri (Heinemann Library, 2004)

Science Answers: Classification by Richard & Louise Spilsbury (Heinemann Library, 2005)

Sharks & Rays of the World by Doug Perrine (Voyageur Press, 2003)

Visual Encyclopedia of Animals (Dorling Kindersley, 2004)

Wild Lives: Swimming with Sharks by Nick Arnold & Jane Cope (Scholastic, 2004)

Websites

BBC Nature
http://www.bbc.co.uk/nature/wildfacts/
Factsheets and articles on different species of fish and ocean habitats.

Enchanted Learning: Zoom Sharks
http://www.enchantedlearning.com/subjects/sharks/
An on-line hypertext book about sharks that allows readers to progress to more advanced information by clicking on links.

The Coral Reef Conservation Program
http://www.coralreef.noaa.gov/
Website of the National Oceanic and Atmospheric Administration's (NOAA) Coral Reef Conservation Program. Information on how people can help to conserve the world's coral reefs plus information on reef conservation.

CRC Reef Research Centre
http://www.reef.crc.org.au/about/index.html
Website of the Cooperative Research Centre for the Great Barrier Reef World Heritage Area. Information is provided about the Great Barrier Reef, the animals that live on the reef, the threats and its conservation.

Seaworld Sharks and their Relatives
http://www.seaworld.org/animal-info/info-books/sharks-&-rays/index.htm/
Information about sharks including an interactive look at shark anatomy.

INDEX

Page numbers in bold refer to a photograph or illustration.